FIRE IN THE SKY

Contents

Jan Burchett
and Sara Vogler

Story illustrated by
Tom Percival

In this story

 Carla

 Rob

 Dad

Introduce these tricky words and help the reader when they come across them later!

Tricky words

- burial
- museum
- enemies
- whistle
- voice
- huge
- lightning
- escape

Story starter

Carla's and Rob's dad is an archaeologist. He finds out about people who lived long ago. One winter, Carla and Rob went with their dad to Greenland to help him find an ancient burial site. Dad hoped to see the Northern Lights while they were in Greenland.

Northern Lights

Carla and Rob helped Dad to set up their camp.

"I think we should find the burial site around here," said Dad, and he and the team began to dig.

"If we are lucky, we might see the Northern Lights tonight," said Dad.

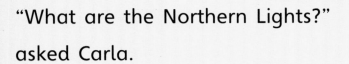

"What are the Northern Lights?" asked Carla.

"The Northern Lights are flashes of beautiful colours that appear in the sky at night," said Dad. "There are lots of legends about the Northern Lights. Why don't you go to the museum to find out about them?"

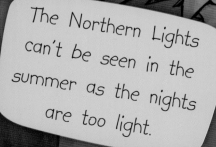

The Northern Lights can't be seen in the summer as the nights are too light.

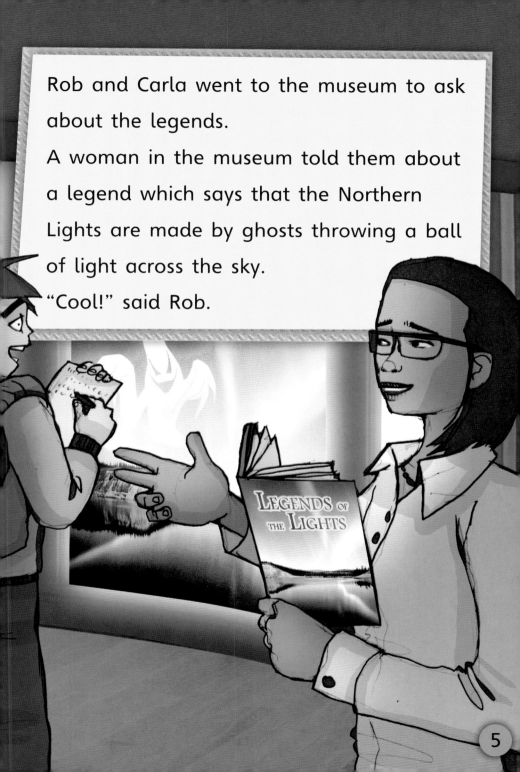

Rob and Carla went to the museum to ask about the legends.

A woman in the museum told them about a legend which says that the Northern Lights are made by ghosts throwing a ball of light across the sky.

"Cool!" said Rob.

The woman told them another legend which says that the Lights are sparks from fires made by ghosts. "The fires are for boiling the heads of their enemies," said the woman.

"Wow!" said Carla.

The woman lent them a book of legends.

Back at the camp, Carla read the book. "Here's another legend," she said. "It says the Lights will dance if you whistle at them." "You must not do that!" said a voice.

Carla looked up.

"I live round here," said a man. "One of our legends says the Lights will be angry if you whistle at them, and they will come and get you!"

"Is that true?" gasped Rob.

"I don't know," said the man. "But I wouldn't do it."

The next day, Dad and his team dug all day but they did not find the burial site. That night they were very tired and they went to bed early.

Carla and Rob lay in their tent. Suddenly, they heard a crackling sound. They ran out to see what it was.

The sky was full of beautiful lights. The lights were green, blue, yellow and red.

"It's the Northern Lights!" said Carla.

"Wow!" gasped Rob. "Do you think the ghosts are boiling the heads of their enemies?"

"Don't be such a baby," said Carla.

"I am going to whistle at the Lights," said Carla.

"Don't do that!" shouted Rob.

But Carla went over to a huge rock and stood on it. Then she began to whistle.

"Come on ghosts!" she said. "Come and get me!" And Carla whistled again. The lights in the sky began to dance. Suddenly there was a very loud CRACK and a flash of light shot out of the sky.

"Look out!" yelled Rob. Carla jumped off the rock. The light hit the rock where Carla had been standing!

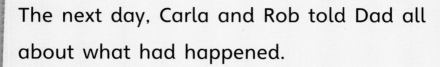

The next day, Carla and Rob told Dad all about what had happened.

"We saw the Northern Lights," said Rob. "But Carla whistled and they came to get us, just like in the legend!"

"The light hit this rock," said Carla. "So could the legend be true after all?"

"No," Dad said, "the Northern Lights could not crack a rock!"

Dad looked at the pieces of rock. "The
rock must have been hit by lightning,"
he said. "You had a lucky escape."
Then Dad moved a piece of rock.
"This is interesting!" he said. "I think the
burial site is here. We must start digging!"

Later that day, Dad showed them a skull he had found under the rock. "Thanks to you we found the burial site," said Dad. "Thanks to the Northern Lights, you mean," said Carla.

"Spooky!" said Rob.

Quiz

Text Detective

- Why did the man tell Carla not to whistle at the Lights?
- Do you think Carla should have whistled at the Lights?

Word Detective

- Phonic Focus: Vowel phonemes in polysyllabic words

  Page 3: How many syllables are there in 'tonight'? Which letters make the long 'i' phoneme?
- Page 12: What words does Carla say?
- Page 13: Find a word that means 'shouted'.

Super Speller

Read these words:

tonight   throwing   angry

Now try to spell them!

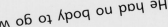

HA! HA! HA!

Q Why didn't the ghost go to the dance?

A He had no body to go with!

Find out about

- Legends about the Northern Lights

Tricky words

- weather
- electricity
- currents
- whistling
- ghosts
- huge
- mouths
- walrus

Introduce these tricky words and help the reader when they come across them later!

Text starter

The Northern Lights are beautiful coloured lights that appear in the night sky near the North Pole. The Lights are made by electricity but long ago legends tried to explain why the Lights appear.

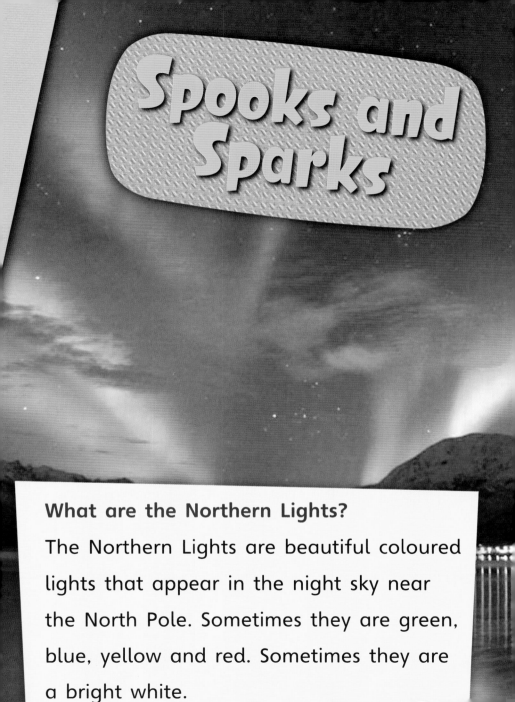

Spooks and Sparks

What are the Northern Lights?

The Northern Lights are beautiful coloured lights that appear in the night sky near the North Pole. Sometimes they are green, blue, yellow and red. Sometimes they are a bright white.

The Lights often look like ribbons of colour that swirl across the sky. Sometimes they look like sheets of colours that twist and turn.

The Lights appear when the weather is very cold and you can see the stars. They only last for about fifteen to twenty minutes each time.

What makes the Northern Lights?

The Northern Lights are made by electricity in the freezing air. Electric currents crash into gases in the air and when they crash, the flashes appear as different colours. Sometimes the Lights make a whistling or crackling sound.

Long ago, people did not know what made the Lights appear and so they made up stories to explain them.

Legends about the Northern Lights

The most famous legend about the Northern Lights says that ghosts make the Lights appear. These huge ghosts live at the top of the world above the lands of snow and ice.

These ghosts are so strong that they can catch whales with their bare hands! But then they need to cook the whales. So they build enormous fires and the Lights we see in the sky are the sparks from the fires as the ghosts cook their supper!

Think how big the ghosts must be!

One grim legend tells how the Lights are made when giants in the sky make fires to cook their meals. But the fires the giants make are not to cook whales but to boil the heads of their enemies!

One legend says that baby dragons are born in the land of the Northern Lights. The Lights we see in the sky are the sparks from the mouths of the baby dragons.

Another legend says that the whistling and crackling sounds are ghosts trying to talk to the people on Earth. If people hear the sounds they should cover their ears. But if they want to answer the ghosts, they should only speak in a whisper or the ghosts will get angry.

The legend warns that people should never whistle back at the Lights. Whistling at the Lights makes the Lights swoop down and snatch the person away, never to return.

Another legend tells of a chief's son who set off to find out why the Lights appear in the sky. He walked for many miles over the frozen sea. At last he got to the land in the sky where he made friends with the people of the Northern Lights.

The people told him that they played football with the skull of a walrus! The Lights are the football being kicked around. When the chief's son returned to Earth he told his people why the Lights appear. He also showed them how to play football!

Some of the legends are funny, some are strange. Today we know why the Lights appear, but it is still fun to read these old stories and to know what people thought long ago.

People travel from all over the world to see the Northern Lights. But are they seeing electric currents crashing into gases in the air, or are they seeing ghosts playing football in the sky?

Quiz

Text Detective

- What does the legend say about whistling at the Northern Lights?
- Would you like to see the Northern Lights?

Word Detective

- Phonic Focus: Vowel phonemes in polysyllabic words

    Page 23: Sound out the five phonemes in 'sparks'. Which letters make the long vowel phoneme?

- Page 19: What do you notice about the words 'bright' and 'white'? Which letters make the long vowel phoneme in each word?

- Page 23: Find six different words which are plural.

Super Speller

Read these words:

should   answer   strange

Now try to spell them!

HA! HA! HA!

Q Why are walruses wrinkled?

 Have you ever tried to iron one?